C is for Cozumel
A Caribbean Alphabet

Written by

Richelle MacKersie

Illustrated by

Franziska Kollewe

Halley Sherwood

Sydney Sherwood

AuthorHouse™
1663 Liberty Drive
Bloomington, IN 47403
www.authorhouse.com
Phone: 1 (800) 839-8640

Published by AuthorHouse 07/19/2019

ISBN: 978-1-7283-1967-4 (sc)
ISBN: 978-1-7283-1968-1 (e)

Print information available on the last page.

Interior Image Credit: Franziska Kollewe, Halley Sherwood, & Sydney Sherwood

This book is printed on acid-free paper.

authorHOUSE®

Dedicated to the people of Cozumel.

The world cannot thank you enough for
allowing us to participate in your daily lives
in order that we may experience your amazing
people, interesting culture, and natural wonders!

A is for **arrecife**, or coral reef! Cozumel is home to the world's second largest coral reef system. In fact, the island was made thousands of years ago when a coral reef grew until it broke the surface of the ocean, and eventually, began to grow vegetation.

The coral we see on the beaches today is actually part of that ancient coral reef system!

B is for beach clubs!

Beach clubs dot the entire coastline of Cozumel. They offer everything from chairs and umbrellas to horseback riding and waterslides!

C is for **corriente marina,** *ocean currents,* and D is for **deriva,** *drifting!*

Although the waters of Cozumel look like they are begging us to jump in and enjoy, they are actually full of strong currents. Drifting in the currents, diving and snorkeling become relaxing ways to explore the world beneath the surface of the ocean. But remember! The longer you drift, the farther back you have to swim...against the current!

E is for El Cedral, the oldest village on the island! This tiny village was once the capital of Cozumel and its largest city. Although the Maya left the island in the early 1600s, a small group of Christian Maya escaped certain death in 1848, by resettling here.

The church they founded still stands next
to one of the oldest Maya ruins on the
island, and the small wooden cross
they brought with them is still inside!

F is for **Faro Celerain Eco Park,** a national park at the southernmost end of the island. By climbing the lighthouse's one-hundred-thirty-four narrow and winding steps, you will be treated to the most magnificent views! The park is also host to lots of unique plants and animals (watch out for the crocodiles and iguanas!), a Maya ruin (El Caracol), and the best beach on the island!

G is for gente, the people, of Cozumel. They are direct descendants of the Maya who have inhabited the area for almost two thousand years! The people of Cozumel still eat some of the same foods, and every house has a Maya mask for good luck and protection. They value family and work very hard at everything they do.

Hamaca is our H!

These traditional sleeping contraptions can be found everywhere! Find one and get comfy swaying in the soft breeze while the ocean crashes on the beach around you.

Iguanas, our letter I, are the squirrels of Mexico! Iguanas are everywhere! They hide in the bushes, run around on the beaches, and dash across streets!

J is for **jungla,** or jungle! Can you imagine discovering this island hundreds or thousands of years ago, before roads and resorts? Using only your hands or a machete, you would have had to slash your way through the impenetrable jungle! But how would you fight off the mosquitos? And how about the snakes?

K is for Ka'na Nah, the Tall House, the only pyramid on the island. Most believe it was the temple used to worship Ix Chel, the Maya goddess of child birth and medicine. According to Spanish explorer Francisco Lopez de Gomara in 1552, the priests would enter a hollow idol from a secret door in the back. Then, they would speak from it to those who had come to worship and beg favors, convincing them the voice came from Ix Chel herself. How sneaky!

L is for **laguna,** or lagoon! Lagoons are plentiful on Cozumel! From the northern lagoons, popular for flat fishing, to Columbia Lagoon in the south, lagoons offer lots of native plant and animal life to see.

Beware! Some of the
permanent residents here
aren't too friendly!

M is for Maya. The Maya of Cozumel were remarkable because they were peaceful, contrary to the Maya on the mainland. They began to settle the island almost two thousand years ago and built villages, temples and even a road system we can still see today!

The Maya also gave us chocolate! Cocoa seeds were so valuable, they used them as money. Can you imagine paying for everything with chocolate?

N is for **negociar**, to negotiate!
Shopping on Cozumel is an adventure all by itself, and negotiating
is the key to success! The locals are shrewd merchants and will start
with "a special price for you, Amigo!" Your mission, should you choose
to accept it, is to negotiate the price down as low as you can. Buena suerta!

O is for the **open-air concerts** held every
Sunday evening in the town square of San Miguel. They
are a wonderful chance to mingle with local families and
experience some real Mexican culture!

P is for **playa**, or beach!
Although Cozumel is known for its
superb scuba diving and snorkeling, it also
has some great beaches! The beaches on the west side
of the island are calmer and have soft sand. Many of them offer
snorkeling right from the shore. Those on the east side are rougher but
less crowded and provide beautiful Caribbean seascapes! Beaches on both
sides of the island are abounding with treasures like coral, seashells, crabs and more!

Isla Holbox

Isla Mujeres

El Ray

Cancun

Playa del Carmen

San Gervasio

Xel Ha

Coba

San Miguel

Tulum

Isla Cozumel

Punta Allen

Key

★ Capital

● City

▲ Ruins

Chetumal

Xcalak

Quintana Roo, our letter **Q,** is the name of the state where Cozumel is located. It was named after Andres Quintana Roo, a politician, author, and lawyer who fought for independence from Spain in the early 1800s. Quintana Roo is the youngest of Mexico's thirty-one states, first becoming a state in 1974.

Andres Quintana Roo

R is for ruinas, ruins, and S
is for San Gervasio, the most
impressive complex of ruins on Cozumel. Ruins
can be found all over the island, but San Gervasio
was once the island's commercial and religious center.
The home of the village leader, temples, and even a building
to house visitors were all located in the central plaza. Every
Maya woman was expected to visit San Gervasio once in her
lifetime to pray to Ix Chel, the goddess of childbirth and medicine.

Tortuga, or turtle, is our letter **T** !
Although turtle meat and eggs were an important part of the Maya diet, sea turtles on Cozumel are now protected.

Loggerhead and green turtles flock to the eastern side of the island in the spring to nest. After they hatch, the baby turtles make a mad dash to the water!

U is for the underwater treasures that are abundant in the waters of Cozumel! Statues of Jesus Christ and the Virgin Mary, a boat wreck, a sunken plane, and, of course, many natural wonders are waiting for you under the sea!

V is for vainilla! The Maya had long been growing and using vanilla when the Spanish arrived in the 1500s. Hernán Cortés took it back to Europe in the 1520s, but the Europeans couldn't cultivate it without the special bees found in Mexico to pollinate it. Finally, in 1841, a twelve-year-old slave boy living on the French island of Réunion discovered that the plant could be hand-pollinated and voilà! Vanilla went global! Even though we can get vanilla everywhere now, nothing beats Mexican vanilla!

W is for the "Wild Side" of the island!
The eastern side of Cozumel is rough and undeveloped.
The waters on this side of the island are full of riptides,
and huge waves constantly crash onto the shores.

The untamed jungle with all of its wildlife
is also still alive and ready to welcome you!

X is for "X" marks the spot!
Rumor has it that pirate Jean Lefitte set up a base of operations in the northern part of the island while it was abandoned. Many believe that this pirate base was on Isla de Pasion. Rumor also has it that his pirate booty is still buried there!

Y is for the Yucatecan cuisine found on the island. Yucatecan cuisine combines the influences of the Maya, Spanish, and other Caribbean islanders. It includes such unique flavors as sour orange, pumpkin seed powder, sweet pepper, achiote, capsicum pepper, and habañero pepper mixed with some more familiar tastes like coriander, oregano, lime, and red onion.

Zocalo, town square, is our letter Z!
The town square is in the middle of San Miguel,
the largest town on the island. There are souvenir
shops, vendors selling their wares, and restaurants.
There are also free concerts every Sunday!

Now that you know your Cozumel alphabet, come and explore for yourself!

My trip to Cozumel

I arrived on Cozumel on _____.

I will stay here until _____.

I'm staying at _____.

I came with _____.

Which coral reefs did you visit?

_____   _____

_____   _____

_____   _____

Which coral reef was your favorite? _____

What did you see? _____

Your pictures

Which beach clubs did you visit?

_____   _____

_____   _____

_____   _____

Which beach club was your favorite? _____

What did you do? _____

your pictures

What unique animals did you see?

_____

_____

_____

What ruins did you visit?

_____

_____

_____

your pictures

Which one was your favorite?

_____

Why? _____

_____

_____

The new things I saw were....

_____   _____

_____   _____

I bought...

_____   _____

_____   _____

My favorite foods were...

_____   _____

_____   _____

My favorite activities were...

_____   _____

_____   _____

your pictures

The next time I come to Cozumel, I want to see...

_____   _____

_____   _____

I also want to...

_____   _____

_____   _____

your pictures

your pictures

Our Team

Richelle, the author and team leader, is an ESL teacher who loves to travel! Two of her four children, Halley and Sydney, and a close family friend, Franziska, illustrated this book. Halley is almost fifteen, a straight-A student, and an avid volleyball player. At twelve-years-old, Sydney is the the youngest on the team. She is also a straight-A student and a dancer. Franziska, a German college student who "joined" our family in 2005, discovered her inner artist while illustrating this book! She is currently finishing up her B.A. in economics.

Richelle and Todd (Richelle's husband) in front of El Caracol at Punta Sur

Sydney enjoying the hammocks at El Mirador

Halley and Franziska being silly after a long day of beach hopping

Printed in the United States
By Bookmasters